Haven't We Met Before?

A Closer Look At Biblical Friends: A Study Series

Katheryn Barlow-Williams

CSS Publishing Company, Inc., Lima, Ohio

HAVEN'T WE MET BEFORE?

Copyright © 1999 by
CSS Publishing Company, Inc.
Lima, Ohio

The original purchaser may photocopy material in this publication for use as it was intended (i.e. worship material for worship use; educational material for classroom use; dramatic material for staging or production). No additional permission is required from the publisher for such copying by the original purchaser only. Inquiries should be addressed to: Permissions, CSS Publishing Company, Inc., P.O. Box 4503, Lima, Ohio 45802-4503.

Scripture quotations are from the *Holy Bible, New International Version*. Copyright © 1973, 1978, 1984 International Bible Society. Used by permission of Zondervan Bible Publishers. All rights reserved.

Library of Congress Cataloging-in-Publication Data

Barlow-Williams, Katheryn, 1960-
    Haven't we met before? : a closer look at biblical friends / Katheryn Barlow-Williams.
    p.   cm.
    ISBN 0-7880-1340-8 (pbk.)
    1. Bible. N.T. Gospels—Biography—Meditations. I. Title.
BS2430.B38   1999
225.9'22—dc21   98-44912
                                                                              CIP

ISBN 0-7880-1340-8   PRINTED IN U.S.A.

*This book is dedicated
to my husband and children
who so powerfully reveal the wonders
of God's grace and love to me.*

Table Of Contents

Preface 7

Introduction 9

Week One 13
   Meet Nicodemus —
   You're Never Too Old To Be Young Again
   Discussion Questions 20

Week Two 23
   Meet The Woman Caught In Adultery —
   Getting Back Up When Life Knocks You Down
   Discussion Questions 29

Week Three 31
   Meet Peter —
   Humility And Faith Hide In Our Pride And Fear
   Discussion Questions 38

Week Four 39
   Meet Pilate —
   Pressured To Give In, But It Isn't Right
   Discussion Questions 44

Week Five 45
   Meet Mary Magdalene —
   To Love Is To Heal, To Hurt, And To Hope
   Discussion Questions 52

Week Six 55
   Meet Christ In Worship —
   Surrender To The Source Of Life, Goodness, And Truth

Conclusion 63

Preface

It's Monday morning. The church newsletter articles are due today, and you realize that you have nothing planned for the next adult education series. You have to write something — and quickly, but what? How about this:

Please join us for a six-week series titled, "Haven't We Met Before? A Closer Look At Biblical Friends." Each week we will visit with prominent gospel characters so that we can develop a better relationship with Christ. Don't miss these great topics:

Week One: "Meet Nicodemus — You're Never Too Old To Be Young Again." Striving for perfection can be deadly — strive for acceptance instead.

Week Two: "Meet The Woman Caught In Adultery — Getting Back Up When Life Knocks You Down." Stop worrying about what other people think and get on with the business of living.

Week Three: "Meet Peter — Humility And Faith Hide In Our Pride And Fear." You don't have to be better than other people to be loved and accepted.

Week Four: "Meet Pilate — Pressured To Give In, But It Isn't Right." Seek God's truth when people are pulling in the wrong direction so that you can be free to live.

Week Five: "Meet Mary Magdalene — To Love Is To Heal, To Hurt, And To Hope." Open your deepest wounds to God's healing love and discover new hope, new life.

Week Six: "Meet Christ In Worship — Surrender To The Source Of Life, Goodness, And Truth." Prayer and meditation open our spirit to God's spirit.

Haven't We Met Before? can be used as a devotional resource for individuals or as a study guide for groups. It was written for busy pastors and church educators who have little time to prepare for an adult education series. Because the curriculum is so easy to use, advance preparation is hardly necessary. As a pastor responsible for Christian education, I am constantly in search of biblically-sound, reality-based curriculum that encourages people to connect their daily lives to the Scriptures. I wrote and used this material for my church's Lenten series one year in an effort to provide a creative approach to Bible study.

Watching the Gospel stories come to life through *Haven't We Met Before?* was not just inspiring, it was fun! It seemed like the biblical characters leaped from the pages and asked the participants, "If Jesus healed my life, don't you think he can touch yours, too?" People listened attentively to the stories, and they shared from the heart. My hope is that busy pastors will breathe a sigh of relief when they pick up this book, knowing that the next six-week adult education series "is in the bag." My prayer is that those who read it will gain a deeper understanding of God's love as they watch the gospel come to life within them and around them.

Introduction

Effective Christian education enables people to connect ancient Scriptures to their lives so that they can experience divine strength today. This curriculum is designed to help the teacher and the student make that connection. Through engaging narratives, biblical characters are introduced as ordinary people searching for divine love. Following each biblical account, a modern voice clarifies how today's men and women can intimately relate to the people of antiquity. As participants take a deep look at the selected readings, they can see themselves. Most importantly they can see the power of God in Jesus Christ which transforms weakness into divine strength.

Haven't We Met Before? allows the reader to see the human side of five biblical characters. Nicodemus, the Woman Caught in Adultery, Peter, Pilate, and Mary Magdalene reveal the feelings and attitudes which can rob people of Christ's joy. Most Sunday school students meet these biblical characters at an early age. However, they meet them as distant people who lived long, long ago, far, far away from contemporary life. They lived so long ago that their experiences don't seem relevant to the stresses of the twentieth century.

But biblical characters are not aliens to modern life. Ancestors of the Christian faith shop at the local grocery store, work in thriving businesses, live in suburbia, and serve in churches today. Countless individuals struggle under the weight of perfectionism, just as Nicodemus did. Many people are burdened with the same shame as the Woman Caught in Adultery. Still others live in a constant lie of rationalization just as Pilate did. Others know the pain of being unappreciated and misunderstood as Mary Magdalene was. Jesus entered into these life-draining burdens 2,000 years ago to proclaim hope. He gave power to the powerless and life to the lifeless.

Through scripture, Jesus still proclaims the power of divine love in the modern world. While personal Bible study is critical for spiritual growth, it does not provide the comfort and the challenge which people can experience in a group setting. The Christian journey cannot be traveled alone. Jesus said, "Where two or three come together in my name, there am I with them" (Matthew 18:20). When people "come together" to the scriptures and honestly share their concerns and joys, they are "in Christ " — "they are a new creation" (2 Corinthians 5:17).

Haven't We Met Before? is designed to help people form a loving circle of support and encouragement. Small groups foster an intimacy that is impossible to capture in corporate worship. When people join together in these intimate settings, the life of the whole congregation is ultimately enriched. Spiritual empowerment spreads throughout the church as people leave their small groups with renewed joy and enthusiasm. In small groups, lonely people are not as likely to get lost in the crowd. They are welcomed into a loving conversation and encouraged to share their experiences. It is only when people talk openly and honestly that they can discover the enormous power of acceptance, compassion, and understanding (Howard Clinebell, *Basic Types of Pastoral Care and Counseling*, Nashville, Abingdon Press, 1988, chapter 14).

Unfortunately, many individuals cannot be open and honest even in church settings. In his book, *Sharing Groups in the Church*, Robert Leslie writes, "It is rather ironic that the church is often the last place where people talk with freedom and openness about the concerns that touch them deepest" (Robert C. Leslie, *Sharing Groups in the Church*, Nashville, Abingdon Press, 1971, p. 14). Though people may be desperately lonely or upset, the fear of being judged or misunderstood is too great for them to speak. They clam up when asked probing questions that touch the heart. As they cross their arms and purse their lips tightly shut, people deny themselves the love and support they need.

Ministers and church educators must encourage participants to open their arms and their mouths so that Christ's love can flow through them. This is no small task. It can be as difficult as trying to feed a child who does not want to eat. How does one get the child to take a bite? Sometimes it can't be done. But occasionally, if the child is really hungry, he or she will eat what is needed.

Sometimes people have to be desperately hungry for divine love before they can open their hearts to receive the gospel.

To help parishioners open up to God and to one another, church leaders must open their own hearts to share the joys and the sorrow of life. They must be honest — at least with themselves — about their own hunger for God. Nothing crushes the spirit of a group more effectively than a leader who refuses to accept his or her humanity. *Haven't We Met Before?* is a study which can help both the teacher and the student accept their weaknesses so that they can discover God's strength within them. It is written for both those who hunger for more of God's truth and for those who are not quite sure what they are hungry for.

Haven't We Met Before? speaks through stories so that participants can see the truth about who they are and discover the freedom to live in a new way, Christ's way. Borrowing from the teaching model of God's prophets, this nonthreatening approach facilitates openness and honesty. Throughout biblical history, the prophets told stories to expose the harsh truths that people tried to deny. When the prophet Nathan told a simple tale about a rich man who killed a poor man's lamb, King David finally confronted his own lust and greed (2 Samuel 12:13). Through simple stories, parables, Jesus helped people see the sometimes painful truth about human nature. The stories in *Haven't We Met Before?* open the heart so that people can share.

Suggestions For Using This Material

Haven't We Met Before? was created as a Lenten series, but it can easily be adapted for other times of the church year. Little advance preparation is needed to use this material in the classroom or in worship. The leader can simply read each session ten minutes before the weekly class. After participants arrive, the leader can choose two readers to present the monologues — one person to read the ancient story, one to read the modern. After the monologues are given, people can divide into groups of six to eight people for the discussion questions.

If the leader has more than ten minutes to plan for a class, he or she can choose dramatic readers to deliver the monologues for each session. A workshop could be held to equip volunteers with the material and to train them to lead small groups.

Discussion questions are found at the end of each chapter which move from the surface level of intellectual speculation to a deeper, spiritual level of personal revelation. It would be impossible to respond to all the questions listed. More than enough are given so the facilitators can choose those which stimulate the most discussion in their groups.

The stories conclude with a worship service so that participants can focus on the ways Christ's spirit has transformed people in the past and will in the future continue to transform their own life stories.

WEEK ONE

Meet Nicodemus — You're Never Too Old To Be Young Again

My colleagues think the new rabbi at the temple is nothing but trouble. This young fellow is peculiar, but no one can deny that there is something special about him. This man they call Jesus has a magnetic power. People flock to him. Even though they have the worst kinds of problems, he doesn't turn them away. With my own eyes, I have seen him heal the sick and comfort the hopeless. I have seen him look at people as if he were looking straight into their soul. On top of all that, he knows more about the Torah than anyone I have ever met. He can answer difficult questions of faith without hesitation. He is an amazing man, but he doesn't ask for praise or recognition. How could anyone so gifted be so modest?

I myself am growing old. I have devoted my life to studying the Torah and interpreting it for others. I always thought if I learned everything I could about the law of God, I would grow close to God. I work with a group of men called the Pharisees. We have been the most respected leaders in the Jewish ruling council for years. There are more than 6,000 Pharisees now, and I help to resolve their questions of faith, legal arguments, and other moral debates. No one could ask for more respect or power than I have. But I have never had what that young rabbi has. The power he has doesn't come from studying books or from the respect of others. It comes from God.

You can see why I wanted to meet him. But I have to admit I was afraid to go to Jesus. Most of my colleagues hate him. I understand their hostility. We've spent our whole lives establishing and following rules that will prepare us for the kingdom of God. And this young know-it-all shows up out of nowhere claiming he can change the world. He says *we* have it all wrong. Try to put yourself in our shoes. If you had worked hard all your life to win the respect of others, would you want to throw it all away? If you had spent your life following God's law, resisting temptation and seeking the truth, would you want to listen to a rebellious rabbi? Who is Jesus to come along and demand that we give up our dignity and act as if we are no better than anyone else?

I have to confess, part of me suspects that Jesus is right. Some Pharisees do care more about personal gain than spiritual growth. But part of me wanted to convince this young teacher that we were not all bad. Most of all I wanted to meet this man who had so much faith, so much peace, and so much inner strength. He didn't seem to be one bit worried what we thought of him. Jesus just taught about God's love and tried to share it with others in need. I wanted that kind of love for God.

So despite my colleague's disdain for Jesus, I went to the place he was staying and introduced myself. I walked into his room and said, "Rabbi, we know you are a teacher who has come from God. For no one could perform the miraculous signs you are doing if God were not with him" (John 3:2).

Then Jesus said the weirdest thing. He said, "I tell you the truth, unless a man is born again, he cannot see the kingdom of God" (John 3:3).

This strange response certainly caught me off guard. I expected Jesus to thank me. After all, I am Nicodemus, a leader of the Jewish ruling council, and I affirmed that Jesus had power from God. Such a young man should be proud and honored that I acknowledged his divine gift.

Jesus didn't seem honored at all. Instead he seemed annoyed. For some reason, as I stood before the young man, I suddenly felt as if I were the ignorant student. Once I stepped into his presence, I forgot that I am a wise, respected religious leader. I didn't know what to say. Jesus was talking in riddles that didn't make sense. I knew about the way to see the kingdom of God. I had studied about such a place and taught lessons on how to live in order to enter God's kingdom. The Pharisees believe that God's kingdom is open to the select few who rigorously follow the divine laws of scripture. We believe that a kingdom of priests and a holy nation will be possible on earth only if everyone knows the Torah inside and out. Before God's kingdom can reign on earth, every person must allow God's law to rule every aspect of his or her life.

In all my years of study, I had never heard anything about being born again, and it certainly did not make any sense. "How can a man be born when he is old?" I asked. "Surely he cannot enter a second time into his mother's womb to be born!" (John 3:4).

Then Jesus said, "I tell you the truth, unless a man is born of water and the spirit, he cannot enter the kingdom of God. Flesh gives birth to flesh, but the Spirit gives birth to spirit. You should not be surprised at my saying, 'You must be born again.' The wind blows wherever it pleases. You hear its sound, but you cannot tell where it comes from or where it is going. So it is with everyone born of the Spirit" (John 3:5-8).

Even though Jesus said I shouldn't be surprised, I couldn't help it. I was dumbfounded. He didn't make any sense. Now if he had told me that God's kingdom would come if I tried harder to be more righteous — that I could understand. But what in heaven's name did he mean when he said, "You must be born again"? And why does he think God's spirit is like the wind? The wind is uncontrollable and unpredictable. We believe that God is predictable. If you do what is right and follow all the laws of scripture, then God's favor will shine upon you. If you ignore the Torah, God ignores you.

I can't tell you how stupid I felt when Jesus asked, "You are Israel's teacher and you do not understand these things? I tell you the truth, we speak of what we know, and we testify to what we have seen, but still you people do not accept our testimony. I have spoken to you of earthly things and you do not believe; how then will you believe if I speak of heavenly things? No one has ever gone into heaven except the one who came from heaven — the Son of Man. Just as Moses lifted up the snake in the desert, so the Son of Man must be lifted up, that everyone who believes in him may have eternal life" (John 3:10-15).

I didn't really understand a word he was saying, except the part about Moses lifting up the snake in the desert. That story was in the Torah so I knew it well. When Moses led the Israelites to the promised land, they had to go through the desert. Exhaustion and lack of food and water threatened to kill the freed slaves. But those who looked at Moses' bronze serpent and trusted in God were saved from death. That night when I went to see Jesus, I didn't understand how Moses' bronze serpent had anything to do with being born again or seeing the kingdom of God.

But the day that Jesus was killed, I saw the law crucify love. Please try to understand, my colleagues weren't all bad. They were simply afraid of this young rebel and his following. They thought he was making a mockery of God's kingdom. He didn't keep good company, he broke the sabbath rules; but worst of all, his popularity threatened to take away their power. We had worked so hard and diligently to win the respect of our people, and now Jesus won their respect even though he was common. How could we give our power over to him? He confused us. He questioned matters that were unquestionable to us. He even publicly humiliated us. Jesus said that the Pharisees do all their good deeds to be seen by people rather than for God. We didn't understand him. We didn't know how to handle him. So we looked to the law and searched our hearts. Then the Jewish ruling council agreed on a terrible decision. They agreed to put Jesus on trial to be crucified.

The day that Jesus went to trial was an awful day. I have never felt so torn between my religion and my heart. Jesus was just a boy with a deep love for God and God's broken, hurting children. He shouldn't have to die. I tried to stop the fury which blazed to kill him. I tried to stop them. Honestly I did. I asked my colleagues, "Does our law condemn a man without first hearing him to find out what he is doing?" I thought maybe if Jesus could just explain himself, then my colleagues would be more reasonable. I had more to say, but they wouldn't listen. They shouted, "Are you from Galilee, too? Look into it, and you will find that a prophet does not come out of Galilee" (John 7:51-52). It was useless. They could not see what I could see in Jesus. They could not believe he was a prophet sent by God. There was no real trial. Their minds were set to kill him.

When I saw Jesus nailed to the cross, his words came back to me: "Just as Moses lifted up the snake in the desert, so the Son of Man must be lifted up, that everyone who believes in him may have eternal life." My own religious colleagues lifted Jesus up on a cross. When I looked at him there, grief, anger, and guilt raged in my soul. If I had spoken up more, done more, maybe I could have stopped this senseless death. Now there was nothing I could do but give him a proper burial. I told Joseph of Arimathea I would go with him to get the body from Pilate when it was all over. When I looked up at the cross, I prayed for the kind of love Jesus had. I prayed for the belief that would give me eternal life.

Jesus said he would be lifted up like the bronze serpent and those who believed in him would be saved. Could it be that if we look to Jesus, our lives will be saved? You can't imagine how hard it is for me to conceive that all I have to do is to trust that that young prophet knows more about God than I do. It goes against everything I have ever learned or taught. How can I stop following the law when that is all I know how to do? From the day I was born, that is all I have ever done. How can I start completely over? Can I learn to believe that God's love is available to me and to others — even if we are not perfect? Is it possible that the law does not have all the answers for our lives? Can I go back and unlearn all that I've learned? Can I in fact be born again?

While these questions swirled in my mind, Jesus' words came back to me. "God so loved the world that he gave his one and only Son, that whoever believes in him shall not perish but have eternal life. For God did not send his Son into the world to condemn the world, but to save the world through him. Whoever believes in him is not condemned, but whoever does not believe stands condemned already because he has not believed in the name of God's one and only son" (John 3:16-18).

Hi! I am Nick. You know me. Some of you know me better than others. I am the voice inside your head which insists that you do everything right. As far as I am concerned, nothing is more important than winning respect and approval. To earn these precious assets, you must work for them. So I am constantly by your side urging you to be the best you can possibly be. When you refuse to take my advice, I poke you with guilt. I know there are times when you don't like me, and you wish I would go away. You would just like to enjoy a hobby, a sport, or your family and your work, but I won't let you. I push you to be the best you can be at any given task. No matter how mad you get when I push you forward, I will not leave.

If it were not for me, where would you be? I give you power. I am the one who makes you work long hours so that your boss will be pleased and your paycheck will grow. I am the one who makes you look your best. When you gain weight, neglect your bills and your housework, I stab you with guilt until you move again. When you want respect, I make you tough so that people fear you. When you want approval, I make you so sweet no one could dislike you. When necessary, I hide your fears, your sorrow, and your anger. As long as I am around no one can see your true feelings. I won't let anyone be offended by your weakness.

People often go to church to seek relief from my exhausting pressure. They think I won't follow them into a sanctuary. But the church does not silence my voice. In fact, it gets stronger when people take up religion. I am opposed to the church's teachings on divine grace and love. Christianity exposes your weakness and claims it can help you. How is humility going to help you in the real world? I try to protect you when you get involved in the church. I stay right by your side urging efficient performance. I help you to focus on the tasks to be done rather than spiritual growth. The church says you are worthy simply because you are a child of God. Come on, you need more than a birth certificate to prove you're okay. You need money in the bank, merit bonuses, awards, sharp clothes, a nice home, and a great car. The church claims that the rain falls on the just and the unjust. I say if you work hard enough you can stay out of the rain and get what you want.

Even though I am a faithful and diligent friend, some of you still want me to move out. I can tell you how to get rid of me. I have never tried to keep it a secret. It's so simple that it's hard for most people to accept. No one wants to give up personal power, and the only way to keep me quiet is to give everything in your life to Christ. When people allow Christ's spirit to live in their hearts, my voice changes. Their relentless striving for perfection gradually stops. They come to believe they are simply a channel of God's love. They quit fretting about the opinions of others, and they stay focused on the grace of God. When Christ's spirit lives within you, my voice can only urge you to enjoy your God-given gifts. Instead of using your talents to prove your worth, you share them to reveal God's love.

I am not afraid to tell you this, because hardly anyone actually gives his or her life completely to Christ. No one wants to give up personal power to receive Christ's power. Though you get sick and tired of my relentless criticism, deep down, you really like me because I don't ask you to give anything. I promise to help you get what you want out of life. From the day you were born, I began teaching you to perform and to seek approval. In school, you learned to prove your worth to your peers and teachers. When you did well, you were rewarded. And when you entered the business world, you joined millions of people who believe that personal worth is based on performance. I have been with you all of your life. There is only one way you could possibly unlearn all I have taught you. You would have to go all the way back to the beginning. You would have to be born again to see yourself and the world through the love of Christ.

WEEK ONE

Discussion Questions

1. Psychologist Howard Clinebell (*Well Being*, San Francisco: Harper/SanFrancisco, 1992, p. 52) states that there are four types of human power, which are:
   a. **power over** — dominance, control of others, often rooted in hidden feelings of impotence
   b. **power against** — attacking, subduing, even destroying others, often rooted in fear
   c. **power for** — nurturing and caring for others
   d. **power with** — mutual empowering through cooperation and collaboration

   Which type of power did the Pharisees practice? Which type of power did Jesus practice? Which type did Nicodemus practice? (You may choose more than one type for each question.)

2. How can these types of power be used in constructive ways, and how can these types of power be used in destructive ways?

3. Think of a time during the last week when you had to give up power — when you had no control of changing a situation to your satisfaction. It can be trivial or significant. For example:
   "I had to stand in the grocery store line for fifteen minutes because the woman in front of me questioned her bill and then the cashier went off duty."

   "After taking a series of medical tests, the doctor said he could still not make a diagnosis. He wants to run more tests this week."

   "No matter how hard I try, I cannot get my _____ (child, spouse, co-worker, parent) to change this annoying habit."

4. How does striving for perfection give you power? How does it deplete your power?

5. How does it feel to give up power? Try to think of both the positive and negative effects.

6. Why was it so difficult for Nicodemus to give up his power? What could he have gained if he gave up his power? Why do you think Jesus told him he would have to be born again?

7. Why is it so difficult for us to give up power? Why is it easier to listen to "Nick" than it is to Christ's love?

8. Have you ever tried to unlearn something about God or personal fulfillment which you once learned at church or school? Was this a difficult process?

9. Jesus said to see the kingdom of God we must be born again. How is Jesus' use of the words "born again" similar and different from the way it is used today? How would you define what it means to a person who had never heard the phrase?

10. Do you try to exert power over certain people or situations, even though your efforts don't change anything? What would happen if you admitted your powerlessness to God?

WEEK TWO

Meet The Woman Caught In Adultery — Getting Back Up When Life Knocks You Down

---

I never intended to let it get this far. One thing led to another and before I could stop it, I was having an affair with a married man. For months I have been struggling with guilt and shame. But I cannot deny myself the passion and the comfort I find with him. For a little while each week, he takes my loneliness away. There is no good excuse for being unfaithful, but please hear my story before you judge me harshly.

When my father arranged my marriage three years ago, I left my hometown to live with my new husband in Jerusalem. I met him on my wedding day. He proved to be a kind but distant man. As long as I manage the household and servants well, he has little to say to me. Most of the time, he is not even here. He stays busy with work and the men in town. Loneliness and boredom drove me to do what I never thought I would. I have no real friends or family in the city and I craved a meaningful friendship. I thought having a child would ease my loneliness, but it did not. In desperation, I went to the temple to seek comfort in prayer. It was there that I met my new friend. From the first time I met him, my heart lifted. This man, who was a scribe, a teacher of God's law, was kind to me. After our first encounter, I began to care again how I looked. Knowing I could see him at the temple made my work at home tolerable. Each morning I rushed to do my household chores so I could meet with him.

I always sat near the back and he would come sit behind me. If anyone else was there, we pretended we did not know each other. It was not acceptable for a Jewish man to talk to a woman in public. Eventually he asked me to meet him privately at his home. His wife had gone to help her sister deliver and care for her baby. I am young, but I am not naive. I knew why he wanted me to see him privately. I knew it was wrong, but I couldn't say no.

In the beginning, it was wonderful. At last, I found relief from the awful ache of loneliness that wrenched my heart. But after a while, the relief turned into guilt. I had broken one of the ten commandments; I defied my God. I planned to end this relationship eventually, but I never dreamed it would happen like this.

As soon as my husband left this morning, I told my maid I had to go to the market because I wanted to choose the fish for our evening meal. Then I rushed to my lover. We were in the bedroom when we heard a group of men pounding at the door. Suddenly a crowd of scribes and Pharisees burst into our room. I tried to pull the covers up, but they jerked them back and told me to get dressed. They said they were taking me to be condemned by Jesus.

I had heard of Jesus but never met him. He was a new rabbi with special powers. I had heard he knew things about people just by looking at them. Did he know I was having an affair? Did he send these men here to get me? That couldn't be. He didn't even know me. When they yanked me out of the house, I thought they would bring my lover with me. But they did not. Even though the law of Moses says that both men and women should be stoned to death if caught in the act of adultery, they did not take him. He was a scribe, and they didn't want to cause a scandal at the temple.

So I faced Jesus and the crowd alone. When they dragged me into the street, unbearable shame and grief pierced my soul. Imagine if your most shameful mistake were put on public display for hostile people to see. I wanted to die, but I didn't want to be stoned to death.

As they dragged me down the street to the temple, I kept my head down. I could not bear to see people glaring at me. They marched me up to Jesus and shoved me on the ground. I stood back up, but I did not dare raise my head. I heard a voice say, "Teacher, this woman was caught in the act of adultery. In the Law Moses commanded us to stone such women. Now what do you say?" (John 8:4-5).

I braced myself because I knew that no rabbi would refute God's law. But then no answer came. I could see a man drawing pictures in the dirt beside me. Was this Jesus? If it was, why was he playing in the dirt? My life was on the line and he was drawing some kind of picture on the ground. This man had to be Jesus because my opponents kept questioning him. Finally he stood up and said, "Let anyone among you who is without sin be the first to throw a stone at her" (John 8:7).

I threw my hands over my face and ducked my head. Every muscle in my body tightened. This was it. The stones would start flying now. It's funny what goes through your head in a crisis. I worried about my little girl. She would be confused when I didn't come home this morning. Now there would be no food for dinner. Other trivial concerns came to mind as the seconds passed. But then nothing happened. I didn't feel anything. Instead I heard the gentle thud of rocks falling in the dirt. I stood motionless with my head covered for what seemed an eternity. Did all the religious leaders have sin? Didn't at least one of them have the right to throw a stone at me?

Then he spoke to me. It was the sweetest, kindest voice I had ever known. Jesus asked me, "Woman, where are they? Has no one condemned you?" (John 8:10).

Cautiously, I raised my head and looked around me. Everyone was gone. "No one, sir," I stuttered, mesmerized by the compassion in his eyes (John 8:11).

"Then neither do I condemn you," Jesus declared. "Go now and leave your life of sin" (John 8:11).

I couldn't believe what he was saying. I was so stunned, all I could do was stare at him. I had broken one of the ten commandments, but he did not punish me nor did any of the other religious leaders. I deserved to be shamed and humiliated, but no one condemned me.

As I stumbled down the street on my way home, I held my head up and looked people in the eye. Some shot looks of condemnation, but others smiled sympathetically. I thought about my husband and how he would react to all of this. He was bound to find out by the end of the day. Even though the rabbi Jesus forgives me, I doubt if my husband or my family can. I have disgraced them. My husband is bound to put me out on the street.

At the same time I was terrified to go home, I was overwhelmed by Jesus' compassion. It was as if he felt my anguish and loneliness in my soul. His words echoed in my thoughts over and over again. "Then neither do I condemn you. Go now and leave your life of sin."

I was ready to leave my life of sin. I didn't even want to see my lover again after what happened today. I was so angry at him. He betrayed me. He said he loved me and cared about me, but when I was in trouble and needed help, he didn't even try to defend me. I wanted to leave him, but where would I go?

How could I face my husband, my family, and my neighbors? I knew I couldn't run away. Maybe my husband would keep me, maybe he would not. But I know my life will never be the same from this day forward. For in one brief moment, the rabbi named Jesus taught me that no one has the right to condemn another human being. We have all done something that makes us ashamed. We all have wounds that cause us to hurt ourselves and others. Jesus gave me the healing power of forgiveness, and I pray that power will get me through the rest of this day.

"Let anyone among you who is without sin be the first to throw a stone at her."

Introductions really aren't necessary. All of you know us. We are the twins named Shame and Guilt. We live inside your mind to help you remember the disturbing moments from your past. Without us, you might forget regrets, mistakes, and shattered dreams. But we hold onto these painful images for you. Though we are similar in many ways, we are not identical twins. I am Guilt. I only jab you with sharp stabbing pains when you have actually done something wrong. I prick your conscience to improve your behavior.

My twin, Shame, on the other hand, can make you feel bad even when you are perfectly innocent. Sometimes his accusations are legitimate. When my piercing stabs do not improve your behavior, Shame weighs heavy in your heart. He holds you down with the dull but constant ache of self-contempt. Most often, however, you are falsely accused by my twin. He blames you for tough luck and bad breaks. No matter how hard you try to be good, shame insists that you are unworthy of love. That awful ache of self-contempt sits in your heart for no good reason.

When I prick you with guilt, you have two ways of reacting to the sting. Sometimes you work even harder to be perfect. Diligently, you hide your faults from yourself and others. You start putting other people down to prove that you are not so bad. You blame your indiscretions on other people. I know. I know. You have told me before. "You were forced to have an affair because your spouse is so boring. You had to cheat on the test because the teacher is too hard. You had to tell a lie because your friend didn't want to know the truth." Someone else is always causing you to stumble.

But then there are times that you just open the door wide open for shame and guilt to enter your thoughts. You don't try to push us away with a defensive protest. Even when we would prefer to leave, you tighten your grip on us. When I prick you with guilt, you instantly recall all of your past transgressions. You seem to enjoy rehashing the morbid details of past regrets. Shame really loves it when you are in this self-loathing mode. Shame thrives on it when you blame yourself because your parents could not meet your needs. He loves it when you feel bad because your significant other doesn't treat you well. When someone looks at you the wrong way and you worry that you have done something horribly wrong, Shame is in his glory.

Shame and guilt are not supposed to dominate your life. Love wants to set you free so that you can enjoy being human. Your mistakes are supposed to be lessons to help you discover the fullness of living. Love wants to transform ignorance into wisdom and harsh judgment into compassion. But it cannot do so unless you can accept your mistakes as opportunities for growth.

Love asks you to accept your own faults, so that you can forgive others. When someone hurts you, love longs to help you forgive and forget. If you cannot forgive, resentment will lash out and push the goodness of life away. Humility could save you from the hostile struggle to prove your worth. But hardly anyone accepts this free gift of love. Everyone wants to be better or worse than his neighbor, never equal.

When you make a mistake or hurt another human being, love longs to spare you from my stabs of guilt and the ache of shame. But you refuse. You think you don't need God's grace, or you think you are too bad to be saved. Until you learn the lessons of love, shame and guilt will rule your heart. There is one who longs to teach you these lessons. He is the Christ who said, "Let anyone among you who is without sin be the first to throw a stone."

In that one statement, Jesus forced people to accept their humanity. No one is any better than his or her neighbors, no matter how religious and pious he or she tries to be. When you accept Christ's liberating forgiveness, shame cannot torture you with the past, nor can guilt pester you in the present. If you confess your sins, God can set you free to love yourself and others.

WEEK TWO

Discussion Questions

1. How are shame and guilt different? How are they similar?

2. Jesus accepted and forgave the woman caught in adultery, but it is unlikely her husband would. Does God's forgiveness and love help you face and deal with people who are rightly angry with you?

3. Does God's forgiveness and love help you to confront and deal with people when they hurt you and make you angry? How so?

4. Why do we like to throw stones at other people?

5. When you feel betrayed by a spouse or a friend, how do you work through it?

6. Why is it so difficult to forgive people? Can you forgive someone who repeatedly hurts you, even after you have confronted that person?

7. Why is it so difficult for some of us to accept forgiveness? How would our lives be different if we did receive God's grace?

8. Why is it so difficult for some of us to admit our shortcomings? How would our lives be different if we did recognize our faults?

9. Do you believe the woman caught in adultery left her life of sin? Do you believe it is possible for people to change after they have consistently pursued self-destruction? If so, what empowers them to change?

10. Are you more likely to blame yourself and beat yourself up when you make a mistake, or do you get defensive? Think about that last time you made a big mistake. How did you handle it?

WEEK THREE

Meet Peter — Humility And Faith Hide In Our Pride And Fear

Terror welled up within me, and I burst out in a rage at those who accused me of lying. Cursing them, I screamed, "I don't know Jesus. I have never met him."

As I was protesting their accusations, a rooster crowed. Its piercing shrill carried the echo of Jesus' words, "Before the cock crows you will deny me three times." In that instant, a silent torture raged within me and I exploded. One second I screamed in outrage, the next I wept in anguish. To those around me, I looked like a madman. They did not understand the rooster's message. But his ominous sound stripped away my dreams, my self-respect, and my hopes for the future (Matthew 26:69-75).

How could I have worked so hard for glory and power, but fallen so hard and so far down? Despite all that I had sacrificed and all that I had learned, nothing had changed. Oh, there had been moments when I was divinely inspired, like the time I announced Jesus was the Messiah, the son of God. Then there was the time when many followers turned away and Jesus asked the twelve of us, "Do you also wish to go?" I was the one who answered, "Lord, to whom can we go? You have the words of eternal life. We believe and know that you are the Holy One of God" (John 6:66-69).

But my moments of divine glory were always short-lived. Maybe they were just good guesses. My revelations never cured my self-delusion. I actually thought I was better than the other eleven. After all, I was the first disciple to be called, and I was the first to recognize Jesus' divinity. But I overestimated my abilities from the very beginning. I talked big because I wanted to be big. How arrogant I was! I wanted to build a house for Elijah, Moses, and Jesus. Who am I to decide where and how God's prophets should live?

In the three years I traveled with Jesus, my pride was wounded a thousand times. I just could not grasp the concept of humility, so pride humiliated me. There are not words to describe the agony I felt when I betrayed Jesus. Once again, I had overestimated my abilities. I couldn't even keep a commitment to someone I loved. When that rooster crowed, reality slugged my soul and knocked me out. It was then I realized that Jesus was right. I was no better than anyone else. Despite my promise that I would never fall away, I fell hard.

The night I turned from Jesus, I ran straight into the arms of despair. In this suffocating grip, I could only regret the dreams of glory which brought me there. At least when I was a fisherman, I never betrayed anyone, and I was never in danger. Yes, my life before Jesus lacked purpose, but it also lacked this heart-wrenching pain. If I had never tried to enter God's kingdom, I would never have found this hell.

That night seemed endless. Remorse would not let me sleep. But morning finally came. Part of me was so ashamed of my failure that I didn't want to see the other disciples. It would be so humbling to admit I was no better than they. If I weren't the best I must surely be the worst. But grief ate away my pride. I could not stand the emptiness alone. The other disciples could share my brokenness.

The eleven of us sorted through our shattered dreams and stumbled through the nightmare of reality. None of us understood how Judas could have turned on us and then committed suicide. We hated the Jews who were responsible for Jesus' death. But most of all we hated ourselves for betraying someone who loved us so much. Because we had nowhere else to go, we went back to our lives of fishing. But it was not the same. We could not forget Jesus, but we could no longer follow him. All hope was gone, so we thought.

None of us remembered that Jesus said he would be crucified and rise again on the third day — until the women came to us with a wondrous tale. Mary Magdalene, Joanna, and Mary rushed to tell us that they had seen two men in clothes that gleamed like lightning.

These men said to them, "Why do you look for the living among the dead? He is not here; he has risen! Remember how he told you, while he was still with you in Galilee: The Son of Man must be delivered into the hands of sinful men, be crucified and on the third day be raised again." (Luke 24:5b-7).

All the other disciples thought that the women had lost their minds, but I had to go see the tomb for myself. I ran all the way there, and found it just as the women said it would be. Jesus was gone, and the strips of linen were left behind. I stumbled home absolutely dumbfounded. Could it be that Jesus was alive? For hours, the scene at the empty tomb haunted me.

Later that same day, two of the disciples claimed they had traveled to Emmaus with Jesus and had dinner with him. Most of us were skeptical. It was just too amazing and wonderful to be true. That night we met at the house of one of the disciples to talk about these rumors. After locking the door behind us to keep the Jews out of earshot, stories began to fly. We were lost in these mesmerizing tales with each of us bursting to share our opinions. But then out of nowhere one voice spoke, "Peace be with you," and silence numbed the room. We turned and gazed in wonder at the face behind the voice. It was Jesus. He showed us the wounds on his hands and side, and we were stunned. This unbelievable miracle threw us all into a state of shock.

Later that evening Jesus left, but he assured us we would see him again. The next day he found us frustrated from an unproductive morning of work. After hours of fishing, we had caught nothing. If we had not followed Jesus' advice, we would have returned home with empty nets. Even though we were exhausted, we did just as he told us. We pushed out farther into the deep water and cast our nets on the other side of the boat. Sure enough, we hauled in more fish than ever, and we celebrated by cooking some right there on the shore.

I remember that day well for more than one reason. On that same morning, Jesus called me once again to serve God. After I had failed so miserably, Jesus still had faith in me. When we finished eating, Jesus asked me, "Simon, son of John, do you truly love me more than these?"

"Yes, Lord," I replied. "You know that I love you." And then Jesus said, "'Feed my lambs."

Three times Jesus asked me if I loved him. Three times I said, "yes." And three times he told me to feed his lambs (John 21:15-19).

I finally understood that Jesus was not interested in grand gestures of pride. All he wanted was a humble act of love. It took me three years to understand that God's glory is revealed in faithful service, not in boastful plans.

About forty days later, Jesus left us for the last time. Once again, we were heartbroken, but this time we were not defeated. He told us to go to Jerusalem where we would receive the Holy Spirit. We followed his instructions and experienced a phenomenal power. But I do not use this power to prove I am better than others as I once would have. I only use it to share God's love with others. This amazing gift of grace has enabled me to do what I could not do on my own. Without this power I could not face the terror of the religious leaders. But now, I do not care what they think. I only care what God thinks.

Just this morning, we went before the Sanhedrin to be questioned by the high priests. They are enraged because we refused to stop healing and preaching in the name of Christ. The Jewish rulers said, "We gave you strict orders not to teach in this name, yet you have filled Jerusalem with your teaching and are determined to make us guilty of this man's blood" (Acts 5:28).

Miraculously, I did not deny anything about Jesus. I proudly admitted that I healed and preached in Christ's name. No one would believe that I was the same man who denied even knowing Jesus. Just two months ago I had cursed people for asking me if I was a disciple. But now I exclaimed without hesitation, "We must obey God rather than men!" (Acts 5:29).

The high priests were so furious they wanted to put us to death. But a Pharisee named Gamaliel, a teacher of the law who was honored by all the people, stood up in the Sanhedrin and ordered that the other disciples and I be sent outside. Later we learned that Gamaliel advised the high priests to let us go. He said if our purpose was of human origin, it would fail. But if it was from God, they would not be able to stop us, they would only be fighting against God.

So instead of killing us, the high priests had us flogged and ordered us not to speak in the name of Jesus. Then they let us go. We left the Sanhedrin rejoicing because we had been counted worthy of suffering disgrace for Christ's name. Of course we did not stop speaking in the name of Christ. Day after day, in the temple courts and from house to house we never stopped teaching and proclaiming the good news that Jesus is the Christ and new life is available for all.

You are living proof that our activity is not of human origin, for the name of Christ has not fallen away even after 2,000 years. Once again, Christ's promise of love has been heard, and each time you share this message in word or deed, you continue our mission.

You can call me Pete, but my real name is Pride. Almost everyone thinks I only cause arrogance, but I can be much more subtle than that. Sometimes I hide behind the sweetest, most innocent faces. Underneath these masks, I am hard at work. I convince you that you are a superior human being who does not need God or friends the way other people do. You are special. You are strong enough to tackle the problems of daily living all alone. You might ask for God's help from time to time, but you do not wait to accept it. At my insistence, you rush off with your own plans and do everything on your own strength. I make you feel in control of your destiny, even though you are not.

Other people might need to lean on their friends and loved ones for support, but not you. You are the strong one. Very few, if any, of your relationships are balanced. You always do the giving because the giver is in control. As the giver, you can decide when and how to give. But to receive is to be vulnerable, at the mercy of others. So I paint you up as a self-sacrificing, generous person. However, underneath that facade, you know you give because it allows you to control others.

Some people say I overestimate your abilities. I like to believe I just accentuate the positive in your life. I get you to take all the credit for your efforts, even if someone did help you achieve your goals. To encourage you, I highlight all the wonderful things you have done, and I project the great things you can do in the future. When you see what I project in your mind, you can't wait to tell other people. You talk about doing these great things all the time, but you don't always follow through. Some of you live in fantasyland and never bring your dreams down to earth. Doesn't matter much though. Talking about yourself makes you feel important and that's all that matters. Oh, sure, you make promises you can't keep. You let people down, but doesn't everybody?

You annoy me with all your fearful complaints. You are afraid that someone will find out that you are not as smart, as brave, or as rich as you say you are. Stop your moaning. Fear is such a small price to pay compared for the notoriety boasting gets you. So what if you are caught exaggerating the truth. You'll think of something to save face.

Yes, I have to admit that every once in a while I get people in serious trouble. But I am not a fickle friend. I stand by you in times of distress. If you are going to put yourself down, I certainly want you to do it well. If you can't live under the delusion that you are the best person among your peers and coworkers, then at least think you are the worst. The positions of best and worst are special. Who wants to admit he is just like everyone else, with faults and strengths?

When you sit in the worst position, you need God's help but you can't accept it. You think you are unworthy of love. You whine and carry on about your shortcomings, but you do not reach out to people who could nurture and support you. Instead you lie down with miserable allies who affirm your self-debasing attitude.

Every once in a while, one of you slips from my grip. You lose a job, a loved one, your health, and you realize that you are not all-powerful or in control. For a while, you blame yourself and accept your lot as the worst. But then something inexplicable happens. Just when you feel completely hopeless and cannot find a reason to go on, Christ lifts you from despair. Divine Love will not accept pride, no matter how well I disguise myself, and it forces me to let you go. Because Christ loves you just the way you are, you can face both the positive and negative aspects of your life. In God's embrace, you no longer need to be the best or the worst. You are content to be a part of the divine creation. Personal limitations and strengths are accepted with humble gratitude, and you find a power not ordinarily your own. In God's embrace you are free to love and to be loved.

WEEK THREE

Discussion Questions

1. What made Peter finally confront his pride?

2. Is it possible to confront pride and rid ourselves of it before it causes considerable pain?

3. Is it ever good to have pride? When does it become harmful to us? How does pride cultivate fear?

4. How can we find a balance between feeling better than or worse than our neighbors? Is it difficult for you to find this balance?

5. Both Judas and Peter were prideful. They wanted to do things their own way. Why do you think Judas committed suicide? How did Peter persevere in light of his failure?

6. What helps us to persevere when we are forced to confront a humiliating failure?

7. Can we discover humility and faith without first having pride and fear? What does a person need to do to receive the gifts of humility and faith?

8. What are some subtle forms of pride? What are some blatant forms? Which is more dangerous to our personal growth and well-being?

9. What media messages promote self-destructive pride?

10. If you could talk to the Bible character Peter, what would you want to ask him about humility and faith? If you could talk back to pride, what would you want to say?

WEEK FOUR

Meet Pilate — Pressured To Give In, But It Isn't Right

It happens occasionally, and sometimes it bothers me, but there's not much to do to stop it. I've seen hundreds of criminals throughout my career. After a while you get a feel for which ones are innocent and which ones are guilty. I don't have much use for the guilty ones — or for the Jews, for that matter. Put them to death, get them out of my hair. But when a convicted man is innocent — it still gets to me.

I am a governor of Rome, and my only real concern is to keep peace in my region. Let's face it, I am no Mister Nice Guy. I'll go to any length to maintain order. I am notorious for violence, briberies, executions without trial, and cruelty to others. But in my region there is order and peace.

I don't have much sympathy for the Jews, so you can imagine how irritated I was when they brought Jesus to me. It was early in the morning and I had hardly pulled my thoughts together. Suddenly I had to deal with a bunch of irate Jews. What did I have to do with a religious squabble? I could care less that this man breaks their laws.

I tried to shrug it all off by sending everyone home, but the high priests persisted. They said that Jesus claimed to be the Messiah, the son of God, which is a crime under Roman law that warrants death. Only the emperor can claim that title. So I reluctantly brought the man into my chambers to talk with him. I suspected that the Pharisees and the Sadducees were just jealous of the fellow. Even I had heard of Jesus and how crowds flocked to see his astonishing powers.

I found Jesus peculiar, but far from dangerous. He was obviously as harmless as a fly. Why kill him when you could ignore him just as easily? When I asked him about what he had done to deserve such hostile punishment, he replied, "My kingdom is not of this world. If it were, my servants would fight to prevent my arrest by the Jews. But now my kingdom is from another place" (John 18:36).

"You are a king, then!" I exclaimed, catching him in the crime of treason.

But his answer did not convict him. It was just another riddle, "You are right in saying I am a king. In fact, for this reason I was born, and for this I came into the world, to testify to the truth. Everyone on the side of truth listens to me" (John 18:37).

Bored and irritated with his responses, I asked, "What is truth?" I didn't wait for an answer. Life is too short to waste it away like a philosopher. What difference could the truth make? It obviously wasn't helping Jesus. If you ask me, this guy should have been less worried about the truth and been more concerned about saving his life.

It was too early to deal with this nonsense, so I decided to let Herod, another Roman governor, do the dirty work. I sent Jesus to be examined by him. Herod was thrilled to meet Jesus because he wanted to see one of his infamous miracles. But Jesus refused even to talk to Herod, much less perform a miracle. Outraged by Jesus' silence, Herod and his soldiers mocked and ridiculed him, then sent him back to me (Luke 23:6-11).

I was stuck with the dirty work and caught in a terrible bind. I didn't want the man to die, but he would say nothing to defend himself. Word had spread all over the region that Jesus was in my custody. When my wife found out about it she went crazy with everyone else. She sent me a note telling me that a nightmare had convinced her that Jesus should be set free (Matthew 27:19). But what was I supposed to do? I tried to win his freedom. It is a Jewish custom to have one prisoner released at the time of Passover. I thought they would let me release Jesus. I called the chief priests, the rulers, and the people and said to them, "You brought me this man as one who was inciting the people to rebellion. I have examined him in your presence and have found no basis for your charges against him. Neither has Herod, for he sent him back to us; as you can see, he has done nothing to deserve death. Therefore, I will punish him and then release him."

So you see, I tried. Honestly, I did try to save this innocent man from being convicted, even though he was a Jew. But the crowd burst into hysteria and shouted, "Away with this man! Release Barabbas to us" (Luke 23:18).

I didn't want to release Barabbas. In my gut, I knew he was guilty. So once again, I went to the crowd who shouted for Jesus' death and asked, "Why? What crime has this man committed? I have found in him no grounds for the death penalty. Therefore I will have him punished and then release him" (Luke 23:22).

But the frenzied hysteria exploded into rage and they cried even louder, "Crucify him! Crucify him!" Finally, I gave in. I gave the crowd what they wanted. I released an innocent man to death to stop the hysteria and to maintain order in my region.

How do I live with myself after turning an innocent man over to the hands of death? It's not so hard. For a while, something strange and mysterious took hold of me and I was haunted by Jesus' crucifixion. But then I remember that I did not kill him. I literally washed my hands in front of that crowd and said, "I am innocent of this man's blood. It is your responsibility!"

And they shouted back, "Let his blood be on us and on our children" (Matthew 27:24-25).

I can live with myself because it was the crowd, not me, who put Jesus to death. Jesus even told me himself, "You would have no power over me if it were not given to you from above. Therefore the one who handed me over to you is guilty of a greater sin" (John 19:11). I am not guilty of Jesus' death. They are! After all, I was just doing my job, keeping order in my region of the Roman Empire.

———————

Hi there! It's been a while since I have seen some of you. But I am sure all of you remember me. I am not the kind of person you can forget. My full name is Rationalization, but a lot of people call me Rat, for short. I don't think my nickname is appropriate, because I am here to help you. You don't always need me, but when you do, I rush to your aid. My primary purpose is to protect you from the painful consequences of the truth.

In my opinion, the truth is highly overrated. Ever since Jesus said, "You shall know the truth and the truth will set you free" (John 8:32), people have sought it. But Jesus failed to mention that the truth can also make you miserable and unpopular. I don't want you to be unhappy or lonely, so I show up at crucial moments to save you. When Christ's truth would have you stand up for justice and love, I make you sit still and keep your mouth shut.

No one can live by the standards Jesus laid down. You try to seek the truth in the business world, and you are bound to fail. Sometimes you just have to do things that are unethical because they are productive and profitable. What's wrong with putting a little extra money in your pocket? Is the truth going to pay your bills and give you the financial security you need? Jesus would like you to believe that. He would like everyone to believe that the truth is more important than a job. But then Jesus didn't have a mortgage payment or kids to send to college either.

My theory is that if everyone else is doing it, you can't be all that bad. So the best way to justify your behavior is to find people who think and act like you do. As long as there is a crowd around, it's hard for Jesus to confront you with the truth. If you have a bad habit like smoking, drinking, or overeating, you certainly want to surround yourself with lots of people who overindulge in similar ways. They can help you squash out the truth when it tries to make you change. If you cheat on your income taxes, you can find plenty of folks to make you feel okay about it. If you are in an unhealthy relationship, it's best to pick friends who are also miserable with their partners. Seeing other people in similar situations makes you feel better about what you are doing.

I know there are times when you desperately want to speak out in truth. You want to stand up for what is right and good and noble. Oh, you would love to speak out against the ills of injustice that plague your home, office, and even your church. Just be forewarned, speaking out can get you into a lot of trouble.

No one wants to deal with problems at work or at home. People want to hear that everything they are doing is at best wonderful, and at worst understandable. Listen to me because I can give you plenty of reasons to keep your mouth shut. Use your voice to tell people what they want to hear. Leave the dirty work of speaking the truth to someone else and go on about your own business.

I say your life should be devoted to meeting your own needs and maintaining a decent appearance. As long as you appear to be loving and kind, what does it matter if you don't always stand by truth? I say when the going gets tough, the truth should get going. Sometimes you just have to bend the rules so that you can save face and maintain the respect of your friends and colleagues. The truth upsets the order of things. It almost always goes against popular opinion. Do you want to be lonely and have your life thrown into chaos? No, of course you don't. So I excuse you from the truth which would alienate you from your friends and family. I give you permission to be ordinary, common, and just one of the crowd.

Jesus wants you to be extraordinary. He wants you to live by divine standards, while the rest of the world lives by human standards. He wants to give you the Holy Spirit which would make you stand against the crowd to defend divine truth. It's fine by me if you want to be extraordinary. Just remember I warned you, "The truth will set you free," but it can also make you miserable and unpopular.

WEEK FOUR

Discussion Questions

1. Did Pilate have a choice? Could he have refused to turn Jesus over to the crowd to be crucified?

2. Why do you think Pilate chose to turn Jesus over to the crowd?

3. Why is it so difficult to stand out against a crowd? How can we get the strength to do so?

4. Why is it so much easier to rationalize our behavior than it is to do what is right?

5. Have you ever been caught up in a crowd and done something you would have preferred not to do? Explain.

6. Pilate tried three times to convince the crowd to listen to him. How can we persist in doing justice when no one wants to listen to us?

7. How do you respond when someone tells a racist or sexist joke? Do you think it is funny? If not, do you hesitate to share your disapproval? Why or why not?

8. Have you ever stood up against a crowd for something you believed in? What happened? How did you feel?

9. Jesus said, "I came into the world to testify to the truth. Everyone on the side of truth listens to me." What makes it difficult to hear Christ's voice? Why don't we listen to him?

10. Pilate responded to the above statement by asking, "What is truth?" How would you have answered Pilate's question?

WEEK FIVE

Meet Mary Magdalene — To Love Is To Heal, To Hurt, And To Hope

---

All these years you have been spreading rumors about me that simply are not true. But now, the lies you have told might as well have been truth. People have thought of me as a prostitute for so long that they cannot believe I was anything else. But I never sold my body to a man. Why do you assume the worst? Just because I am a single woman who is not a slave, everyone thinks I make a living in the sack. But there are other ways a single woman can survive in Galilee. They're just not as exciting as the sordid reputation of a prostitute.

Perhaps the rumors began because I do have a strange and shaded past. Just a few years ago, I was possessed by seven demons. This probably sounds bizarre to you. But demons are not as rare as you might think. In fact, you have probably been touched a time or two by the demons who strangled me. These evil spirits are known in your world as fear, shame, rage, guilt, paranoia, loneliness, and self-contempt. Under their demonic force, I did things I would normally not do. Their torment was so awful that I screamed hysterically in public places. I lashed out at people who had done nothing to me, and I beat myself to make them go away. But nothing I did drove the demons away. I only succeeded in driving the people I needed away.

So how did I survive? When the demons weren't attacking me, I worked with friends. We sold things like spices, sesame seeds, fish, and vegetables in town. When the demons attacked, I lay at the mercy of others and I begged for food. But as far as I can remember, even when I was in the grip of a demon, I never accepted money for sex. It's easy to see how the rumors began, though. As a woman who was neither married nor a slave, I had no rights. I had no right to refuse a man who wanted to take me to his bed. I was available to anyone who wanted me, not because I had no moral convictions, but because I had no right in my society to say no. I suppose people thought the men paid me for my services, but they did not.

You may wonder how I came to live like this, but I have few answers. There is no family to tell me about my childhood. Depending on how you look at it, I was either lucky or jinxed at birth. I survived infancy. Most babies in my situation would not have. In my society, a baby has even fewer rights than a single woman. There are no advocacy groups for child welfare. There are no orphanages for unwanted children. It is the father, or the man of the house, who determines if a baby will be kept and raised. The mother does not have a say in the matter. If the mother gives birth to a healthy son, he is always kept. However, if the son is not healthy, or the mother has a daughter, the man of the house decides to keep the baby or to leave it outside until it either dies or someone claims it to raise (*The Women's Bible Commentary*, Westminster/John Knox Press, 1992, pp. 393-394).

I imagine that I was left outside to die, but somehow I survived. Childhood memories have evaporated from my mind. The demons absorbed most of them. But bits and pieces of the past occasionally surface in my thoughts. I recall working in one household and spinning wool. And I remember the day I was thrown out of that house because of my uncontrollable fits.

I don't know how long I lived on the streets before I met him. But I do know that the evil spirits would have eventually killed me had it not been for Jesus. His love was so strong that the demons could not stand against him. When Jesus looked at me with that mysterious glow of love in his eyes, the demons fled, and I was free. Love shattered the fear, the shame, the rage, and the self-hatred, and a new life arose from the broken pieces of my past.

Jesus was the first man I had ever met who touched me with compassion and not abuse. He just wanted me to know that I was loved. When he asked me to join him and the disciples on their travels, I was afraid. What if the disciples wanted to hurt me? What if the demons came back and I wasn't near my own town? What if I couldn't survive? But then I met the other women who were traveling with Jesus. Joanna, the wife of Cuza, the manager of Herod's household; Susanna; and many others. They all spoke so highly of these men, I knew I had to go. We supported Jesus and the disciples out of our own means. Some of the women who traveled with us were wealthy. Others, like myself, collected and sold things to raise money for the cause (Luke 8:1-3).

The years I traveled with Jesus were the happiest years of my life. The disciples and the women were like brothers and sisters to me. For the first time ever, I had a family who loved and cherished me. They were not afraid of my past, nor of the demons which once haunted me. Their faith inspired me to believe in my own goodness. Serving Jesus was my greatest joy. I loved hearing him speak about the wonders of grace, and I loved telling others all he had done for me. Nothing was more mysterious or wonderful than watching him heal and transform broken lives. It was such a comfort to watch Jesus cast demons out of other troubled souls. It made me realize that I was not alone anymore. There were others who experienced the pain of my past and the joy of my transformation. The love of Jesus literally fed us and brought us back to life.

But his love also frightened people. The Sadducees and the Pharisees were terrified of his empowering love. They were afraid Jesus' power would rob them of their own authority. You know the story they fabricated to have him killed. I had been tormented by seven demons all my life, but the pain of seeing Jesus on a cross hurt worse than those demons. I watched the crucifixion from a distance with some other women. Anguish wrenched my soul and tears spilled uncontrollably from my eyes. My Lord, my Lord, my Lord of love was dying and I could do nothing to stop it. Oh, everything in my being wanted to save this man who had saved me from death, but there was nothing I could do.

So we watched and we waited until they finally took his body from the cross and placed him in a tomb. Grief settled so deeply within me that I could not eat or sleep. In desperation, I went out to his tomb in the dark hours of early morning. When I got there, panic stabbed at my grief. Something was wrong. The stone was removed from the entrance. I rushed away to tell the other disciples that someone had robbed our tomb. Peter and I ran all the way back, and he went in and found the grave empty. Everyone was astonished. Who would take Jesus' body? I was heartbroken.

All I wanted to do was give Jesus a proper burial, but now I couldn't even do that. The other disciples eventually returned to their homes, but I stayed. I couldn't move because I could not stop sobbing. I kept looking in the tomb, as if Jesus would be there if I just looked harder. But then the strangest thing happened. At one point I looked into the tomb, and I saw two men sitting where Jesus' body had been, one at the head and the other at the foot. They asked me, "Woman, why are you crying?"

I said, "They have taken my Lord away, and I don't know where they have put him." Then I turned around and I saw another man who asked, "Woman, why are you crying? Who is it you are looking for?"

I thought he was the gardener and might know what had happened to Jesus' body. I cried, "Sir, if you have carried him away, tell me where you have put him, and I will get him" (John 20:10-15).

But then the man I thought was the gardener spoke my name. It was the same voice I heard the day Jesus healed me. "Mary," he said.

And suddenly I knew it was he, my Lord, my Savior. "Rabboni!" I exclaimed in wonder, and I reached to hug him. But he stepped back and said, "Do not hold on to me, for I have not yet returned to the Father. Go instead to my brothers and say to them, 'I am returning to my Father and your Father, to my God and your God' " (John 20:16-18).

I desperately wanted to cling to Jesus. I didn't understand why I couldn't hold on to him, but I had learned in my travels that faith calls us to do things we don't understand. Reluctantly, I left to tell the disciples that Jesus is alive. I had seen the Lord! All hope was not gone. But none of them really believed me. They thought I was just out of my mind again. I knew the truth, though. I knew that Jesus had come back. Death is not the end. After Jesus appeared to the disciples, they never again questioned my sanity. From time to time, the demons try to grab hold of me again, but the love Christ gave me lives today. And that love casts out the evil spirits which you call fear, shame, rage, guilt, paranoia, loneliness, and self-contempt.

No, I was never a prostitute, but I was a woman tortured by a painful past until Jesus handed me the gift of new life. It is a gift available to everyone, and nothing — not even death — can take it away.

Hello, you stupid weirdo, how have you been? You'll never forget who I am because I talk to you all the time. I am your old buddy Failure. Now, what would you do without me at your side? I excuse you from the fear of risks and the pressures of living. When you try to change for the better, I am on the spot with a mirror of your past and a looking-glass into the future. The mistakes of yesterday reflect tomorrow's misery. Oh, sure, go ahead. Try a new job or an interesting hobby. I'll hold up the mirror of misery so that you can stop dead in your tracks. When you see all the projects you have started and never finished, you are so overwhelmed you can't be bothered with another one.

Even if you manage to achieve some noteworthy accomplishment (which, by the way, most everyone does), I won't let you enjoy success. Instead I unleash the phantom "Fraud Squad" in your head. The Fraud Squad is an imaginary committee who is out to prove your incompetence. By employing self-defeating tactics, the Fraud Squad can render you worthless. It will make you too fearful to ask legitimate questions, and too nervous to stand your ground. Even if 100 people praise your work, the Fraud Squad can make you obsess about one person's criticism. It's not hard to spoil your success.

But if for some reason you are able to escape the Fraud Squad at work, I'll send them to your home. If you are doing well at the office, something must be amiss in your personal life. The Fraud Squad will shriek at your piles of endless laundry, the dishes in the sink, and the lack of time you have for your family. What a loser you are.

When you decide to go on a diet, or some other equally obnoxious self-improvement program, I help you relax. With the slightest deviation from your goal, I lead you to oblivion. I am the one who makes you see that if you eat one cookie you might as well have a dozen. If you missed your morning exercise today, I quickly announce that you are a big fat slob who will never stick with a regular exercise program. See how good I am at making you feel like dirt when you really haven't done anything wrong?

Life hands me so many good resources to make you feel worthless. When you get sick, or notice that you are getting older, I can have a field day. No one expects you to keep your spirits up and to participate actively in life if you are sick or old. If your body fails you, then you are a failure — at least that's what you like to hear. When you dwell on your aches and pains you are excused from a positive attitude and productive life. After all, only young and healthy people can enjoy the good life.

And when it comes to relationships, I am quick to remind you of the many times you have been hurt or disappointed. It's so much better to be a loner than it is to trust people. Love doesn't heal. Love hurts. The closer you get to someone, the more it is going to hurt when that person leaves. All relationships have to come to an end one way or another. But if you never get close to someone, you never have to feel the deep pain of grief. A little loneliness today spares you from the inevitable agony of loss tomorrow.

You pretend to hate me, but I know you don't. You relish my constant diatribe because it excuses you from the business of living. If you are worthless, who can expect anything from you? To stop others from criticizing you, you let me shoot you down first. If you got rid of me, you might just have to start taking responsibility for your life. You would certainly need to start standing up for yourself — set some boundaries and confront the people who have been abusing you all these years. And that would take so much energy. So give it up.

Now, I'll be the first to admit that I stretch the truth when it comes to your worthlessness. But if you wanted to hear the truth, you would listen to Jesus. To silence my endless chatter, you could repeat Bible verses and affirmations about God's love. You could spend time in prayer and meditation, earnestly seeking ways to use your spiritual gifts. If you truly believed that you were a friend of Christ, you could not listen to me. You would be too busy sharing the good news of God's healing love. But all that takes such effort.

Jesus says that you are a winner simply because God created you. But it's a lot easier to listen to me and do nothing than it is to live like a winner.

WEEK FIVE

Discussion Questions

1. Think of a time when a first impression of someone turned out to be false. How long did it take to reshape that impression? Why do first impressions have such powerful impact on us? Why do people assume Mary Magdalene was a prostitute?

2. Do you have any impressions of yourself that are false? Is your self-image based on past mistakes or on current possibilities? Why is it so hard to reshape our impressions of ourselves?

3. Do you believe Christ can cast out the demons which torture us: fear, shame, rage, guilt, paranoia, loneliness, and self-contempt? What must we do to have these removed from our lives? Do they ever leave us completely?

4. When Mary discovered that Jesus was alive, she wanted to cling to him, but he told her to let go. He instructed her to go tell the disciples he was alive. Have you ever had to let go of something because faith called you to do so? What was it? How did you feel after you did it? How do you think Mary felt?

5. After the disciples and Mary discovered the empty tomb, the disciples went home and Mary remained sobbing. How do you think you would have reacted? Why do you think Mary was crying? Why do you think the men left?

6. What are some reasons that we don't take the time to talk and listen to Christ? What else do we do with our time? Does prayer and meditation feel like an inefficient use of time?

7. Does prayer and meditation always make you feel better? Why or why not?

8. Why is it so hard for many of us to "rest"? What helps you to relax and to release your worries?

9. Why do you keep going back to old habits and methods of coping that we know don't work? Why does it take us so long to leave our concerns in God's hands?

10. The disciples and the other women who followed Jesus became a family to Mary Magdalene. What are some characteristics of a healthy family? What are the characteristics of a dysfunctional family? How can we create a healthy family for ourselves through the church?

WEEK SIX

Meet Christ In Worship — Surrender To The Source Of Life, Goodness, And Truth

Repentance And Renewal
Worship Service

CALL TO WORSHIP

Leader: The minute we wake up in the morning we begin to write a story. As soon as our feet hit the floor, our thoughts spin a tale about who we are and what we must do to get through the day.

People: In the rush to conquer our daily tasks, we forget that we belong to God. Instead of greeting each new day with joy and gratitude, we face the day with a knot in our stomach. We wonder how we will get it all done.

Leader: Christ came to tell us a story of God's transforming power. When we listen closely, fear is transformed into faith, resentment is healed in forgiveness, and petty bickering is calmed by compassion.

People: We cannot heal ourselves. We need Christ's love so that we can change our story to God's story and live in new ways.

Leader: God's story is told on earth each time we slow down and ask Christ to fill our hearts with love. Let us now join in prayer so that we can once again listen to God's story of love.

INVOCATION *(unison)*
Dear God, you alone can calm our fears and love us back to life. In this hour, breathe your divine spirit into our human spirit. Unleash the winds of new life and set us free to live passionately and joyfully. Oh, powerful Redeemer, we ask you to change our thoughts so that we can live in peace with ourselves and with others. May your kingdom truly come as we seek to carry your love into our homes, our workplaces, and our schools. May our very lives proclaim your great story of love. In Christ's name we pray. Amen.

LITANY OF CONFESSION AND FORGIVENESS
Leader: Like Nicodemus, we struggle to find answers. We try to make our lives work, but we can't. The winds of Christ's spirit push us toward new life, but we are afraid to go. What will we have to give up? Where will God take us? How do we give up control?

People: Jesus, we need you. Set us free.

Leader: Like the Woman Caught in Adultery, we are embarrassed and ashamed of our behaviors. Instead of following Jesus' command, "Go and sin no more," we are stuck in the misery of regret. We cannot "go" anywhere because we are imprisoned by self-condemnation and the judgment of others. We cannot accept Christ's forgiveness and love.

People: Jesus, we need you. Set us free.

Leader: Like Peter, we strive to be good, strong people of God. And we hate our faults so much that we deny them. We judge other people so we don't have to judge ourselves. We set impossible standards, and when we fail to meet them, we are devastated. We feel worthless, and we want to give up on faith. It's so hard for us to believe that we don't have to be perfect to be loved.

People: Jesus, we need you. Set us free.

Leader: Like Pilate, we are often faced with difficult choices. We desperately want to do the right thing and stand up for our convictions. But when the truth calls us to speak against our bosses, co-workers, or loved ones, we remain silent, or lie so that we can tell them what they want to hear. The truth is lost in our rationalizations. How quickly we exchange self-respect for the approval of others, when nothing but God's approval matters.

People: Jesus, we need you. Set us free.

Leader: Like Mary Magdalene, we have known emotional turmoil and the deep grief of loss. We have stumbled through days of confusion and sorrow. There are times when life hardly seems worth living and we wonder how we can go on. We mourn, but we don't feel blessed because there is no one who can comfort us.

People: Jesus, we need you. Set us free.

ASSURANCE OF PARDON
Leader: My friends in Christ, listen to this good news: Christ can do for us what we cannot do for ourselves. In Christ we find the willingness to surrender, the strength to move on, the humility to accept ourselves, the courage to speak the truth, and the love we need to heal. In Christ we are indeed new creations. Do you believe Christ's miracle of new life awaits you?

People: We believe in Christ's promise of new life. We now offer our lives to God's redeeming love so our lives will tell God's great story of love.

SCRIPTURE
Matthew 6:25-34

MEDITATION
Hello. It's been so long since we have had the chance to sit down and really talk. I know you are so busy. You have so many chores to do, projects to finish, and people to care for that you

haven't had time for a long conversation. The best you have been able to do is to wave a quick hello or good-bye when you rush past. So many times I have wanted to say, "Come to me, you are so tired and overburdened. Let me give you a moment's rest." But I knew if I tried to talk with you, I would only be wasting my time.

You've been consumed with other people and their suggestions. You don't have time to listen to me. Now, don't get defensive. I am not blaming you. I know how much you want to be respected by your colleagues and loved by your friends and family. Of course you want to look and be your best. And your old friends claim they can help you achieve personal excellence. I noticed you talking with Nick the other day. He must have told you to strive for perfection in all you do. According to him, anything less than perfect is unacceptable. After people visit Nick, it's not long before they see the twins, Shame and Guilt. They won't let you forget your mistakes, so you know you are not perfect, even though Nick said you had to be. When I saw you with the twins, I knew who you would visit next. Naturally you went see Pride. Pride tells you how to cover up the wrongs you have done — deny your shortcomings or blame them on others. And finally you went to Rat's house. You can call Rationalization by his nickname, Rat, because you know him so well. He helped you come up with good excuses for doing the things Pride told you to do. But ultimately you wound up with Failure.

None of them worked, did they? Oh, they helped you feel better for a little while, but then the demons of loneliness, fear, sorrow, and resentments come back even stronger than before. I couldn't help you while you were rushing from place to place. I knew you would not listen to the voice of love until you were ready. Finally you are here. Tell me where you hurt ... Give me your tears ... What are you afraid of? ... Why are you angry? ... Why do you feel so bad about yourself?

I know that living with me is not easy. It is sometimes hard to hear my voice amidst the chatter and confusion in your mind. I don't give you answers as quickly as you would like, and people often jump in and tell you what you want. I don't always tell you what you want to hear. Sometimes I do ask you to change radically the way you see yourself and your world. But you would rather hang on to what you have always known. When you ask me for mercy and forgiveness, I hand it out to you, but then you refuse to take it. You would rather feel bad about yourself than accept my free gift of grace. I want you humbly to admit your weaknesses and your strengths so that my love can transform your life. But pride won't let you tolerate weakness. It makes you struggle to prove your worth. I want you to know that I am with you, even when you have to make unpopular decisions and everyone turns against you. I want you to believe that you are lovable even when others don't like you. But you insist on seeking people's approval because you believe they can help you to accept yourself.

You trusted the others, Nick and everyone else, but they failed you. So now I beg you, please give me your life so that I can embrace it with love. I will not fail you. Through me, you will discover more love and joy than you ever dreamed possible. It is true that there will be times when you stumble through difficulty and struggle to bear the weight of a cross. But with me, doubt, confusion, and despair are transformed into faith, peace, and joy.

I am here to set you free. You do not have to listen to the conflicting voices in your head. "Be still and know that I am God" (Psalm 46:10). Listen to my voice of love as it whispers these words into your heart.

• Live only in today. Leave your regrets in the past where they belong. Cast your worries of the future aside. Enjoy the wonder of each new day. It is a miraculous gift of life.

• Stop seeking the approval and attention of others. Live in my love and share it freely. Accept that some folks will love you for no good reason, and others will dislike you for no reason.

• Know that each mistake you make is a valuable source of wisdom. Lighten up on yourself and remember you are human. Only God is perfect.

• Laugh often. Don't take yourself so seriously that you can't enjoy the humorous side of life. It is there, if you look for it.

• Believe that your needs will be met. Your employer is not God, nor is your bank account. Spend your money faithfully and wisely. If your needs are being met today, thank God and stop worrying about the future. If your needs are not being met, pray for guidance and act in faith.

• When disappointment or tragedy strikes, know that I am with you. Try not to blame yourself or God. Accept responsibility only if you are in fact responsible. Regardless of your part in the situation, hold on to your faith. Let love guide you through the pain.

• Know that I am always with you. I often speak through other people. Don't deny your hidden pain. Share your burdens with me and with those you trust. And have compassion for those who need you to listen with my love.

• When you are exhausted, overwhelmed, or terrified, be still and listen for my voice. And you will hear these words whispering in your heart: "Come to me, all you who are weary and burdened, and I will give you rest. Take my yoke upon you and learn from me, for I am gentle and humble in heart, and you will find rest for your souls. For my yoke is easy and my burden is light" (Matthew 11:28-30).

OFFERING
Let us now offer our gifts and our lives to God's redeeming love.

PRAYER
Dear God, we pray that you would use these gifts to proclaim your great story of divine love on earth. May our gifts speak of your love and your power as they touch those in need. And, God, we pray that you would use our very lives to tell your story of love on earth. Speak through us in everything we say and do, that others might hear of your great love for them. In Christ's name we pray. Amen.

CHARGE TO THE CONGREGATION
The choices we make today, the way we treat people, the work we do, and even the thoughts we think will tell a story. Through faith, you have the power to make it a story of love, hope, and endless possibility. For that is Christ's story.

BENEDICTION

And now leave this place convinced of these truths: God your Creator is always with you; Christ your Redeemer will pick you up should you stumble and fall; and the Spirit your Sustainer will give you the strength and courage you need to live out your life story in love. Amen.

Conclusion

Jesus came to earth to tell God's story: divine love can redeem the broken and shattered pieces of human life. In this story every man, woman, and child is called to play a vital role. How do we join in this miraculous tale of life, death, and resurrection? We begin by accepting our part with gratitude.

There are people, even dedicated church folks, who waste their chance to speak for God. It's easier to mourn our past and to fear the future than it is to get on with the business of living. Everyone is capable of being miserable. But it takes faith and spiritual discipline to bring God's story to life.

Jesus didn't leave his followers on earth to make them miserable. He left them here so that they could joyfully tell God's story of love. And somehow, that ill-sorted group of men and women pulled themselves together to do their part for God. The apostles proclaimed the gospel even when they were beaten, stoned, and imprisoned for their beliefs. They looked straight into the face of despair and preached about hope and the endless possibilities created with each new day. Regardless of how miserable their circumstances were, they saw God at work within them and around them.

Jesus did not leave us in this world to be miserable. We are here to tell a story — not just our story, but the story of a God who transforms sorrow into joy. When the tattered pages of our lives are collected into divine love, they are given meaning and purpose. Many of us are so focused on the tattered mess before us we cannot see that our little stories can easily fit into a chapter of new life.

Nicodemus, the Woman Caught in Adultery, Peter, Pilate, and Mary Magdalene have told their stories about Jesus. Not all of them ended in radical transformations. We don't know if Nicodemus ever left the pious and misguided Pharisees. And it is almost certain that Pilate never accepted his part in Jesus' death. Who knows if the Woman Caught in Adultery truly left her life of sin? These three biblical characters teach us that perfectionism, rationalization, and even shame are life-threatening. But we are not without hope. Mary Magdalene and Peter proclaimed that old ways of thinking and acting can indeed be forever changed by Christ's love. A passionate spirit filled them with such courage and joy that they could not be stopped from telling God's story, even when people thought they were insane.

The story must continue. It is now our turn to speak for God. Instead of quoting scripture and verse, we need to live the gospel. When we show up for work without the harsh whip of perfectionism, Christ's peace enters the office. When we can forgive ourselves and others for hurtful mistakes, God's grace heals our relationships. When we no longer need to prove our superiority, a quiet confidence dismantles insecurities. When we stop rationalizing and blaming others for our faults, the truth sets us free to live in new ways. And finally, when we can be vulnerable enough to admit that we are hurt and confused, Christ's healing power is unleashed.

Jesus left his disciples with this promise: "I tell you the truth, anyone who has faith in me will do what I have been doing. They will do even greater things than these ..." (John 14:12).

Jesus has left us here to do what he did: to tell the story, God's story, and when we tell that story through our day-to-day tasks, we will be amazed because "even greater things than these" will unfold miracles of grace, hope, and new life.

www.ingramcontent.com/pod-product-compliance
Lightning Source LLC
Chambersburg PA
CBHW071756040426
42446CB00012B/2577